Sam, Dan and Nat

Sam

Dan

Nat

Sam sips it.

Dan sips it.

Nat sips it.

Sip, sip, sip.

Sam, Dan and Nat
Level 1: Story 1

Before reading

Say the sounds: s a t p i n m d
Ensure the children use the pure sounds for the consonants without the added "uh" sounds, e.g. "mmmm" not "muh".

Practise blending the sounds: sip Dan Nat Sam sips

High-frequency words: it and

Vocabulary check: sip – to drink with small mouthfuls

Story discussion: Look at the cover. Who will this story be about?

Teaching points: Make sure that children know that the sounds for both lower case and capital letters are the same. Explain that capital letters are used in people's names and use children's names as examples to show this.
Talk about the verb "sip" and how with the addition of "s", it becomes "sips".

After reading

Comprehension:
- Who did we meet in this book?
- What is the girl's name and what are the boys' names?
- Do you think they are brothers and sisters? What makes you think that?
- Where do you think they might live?

Fluency: Speed read the words again from the inside front cover.